THIRD GRADE BOOK:
I Love Science

SPEEDY PUBLISHING LLC

Speedy Publishing LLC
40 E. Main St. #1156
Newark, DE 19711
www.speedypublishing.com

Copyright 2015

ISBN: 978-1-6814-5448-1

First Printed 03/23/2015

Planets

MERCURY

THE SOLAR SYSTEM

Mercury

Mercury is the closest planet to the Sun and due to its proximity it is not easily seen except during twilight.

A year in Mercury is just 88 days long.

Mercury is the most cratered planet in the Solar System.

Venus

Venus is the second planet from the Sun and is the brightest object in the night sky after the Moon.

A day on Venus lasts longer than a year.

Venus rotates counter-clockwise.

VENUS

THE SOLAR SYSTEM

MOON

EARTH

THE SOLAR SYSTEM

Earth

Earth is the third planet from the Sun and the largest of the terrestrial planets.

The Earth has the greatest density.

It is where we live!

Mars

Mars is the fourth planet from the Sun. Named after the Roman god of war.

Mars is home to the tallest mountain in the solar system, the Olympus Mons.

MARS

THE SOLAR SYSTEM

DEIMOS

PHOBOS

Jupiter

The planet Jupiter is the fifth planet out from the Sun, and is two and half times more massive than all other planets.

Jupiter has the shortest day of all the planets—9 hours and 55 minutes.

Saturn

Saturn is the sixth planet from the sun and the most distant that can be seen with the naked eye.

Saturn is the flattest planet

Saturn has the most extensive rings in the solar system.

SATURN

THE SOLAR SYSTEM

IAPETUS

TITAN

RHEA

DIONE

TETHYS

ENCELADUS

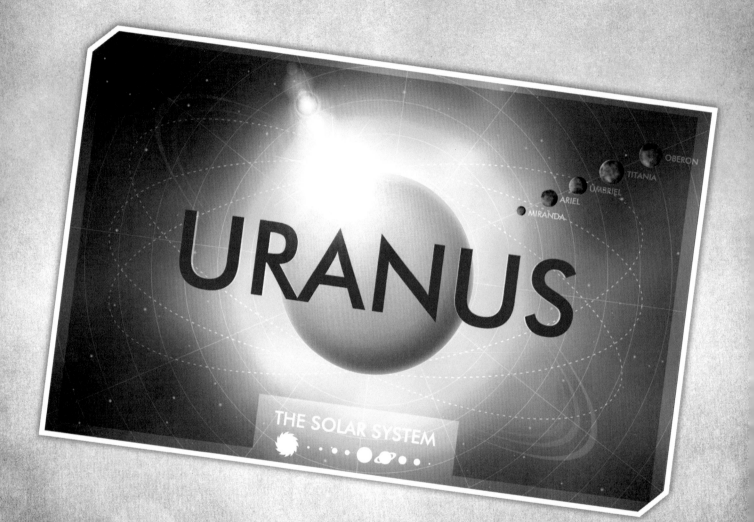

URANUS

THE SOLAR SYSTEM

Uranus

Uranus is the seventh planet from the Sun. It's not visible to the naked eye, and became the first planet discovered with the use of a telescope.

Uranus turns on its axis once every 17 hours and 14 minutes.

Neptune

Neptune is the eighth planet from the Sun and is the most distant planet from the Sun.

Neptune has a very active climate.

It has 14 moons.

NEPTUNE

TRITON

THE SOLAR SYSTEM

PLUTO

THE SOLAR SYSTEM

CHARON

NIX

HYDRA

Pluto

The no longer major planet since 2006, Pluto is now considered a dwarf planet instead.

Pluto has 5 moons.

No spacecraft have visited Pluto.

SECTION ACTIVITY

Arrange the planets from the 1st closest to the sun to the most distant.

1. _____   5. _____

2. _____   6. _____

3. _____   7. _____

4. _____   8. _____

Jupiter   Mars

Venus   Mercury

Neptune   Saturn

Uranus   Earth

Animals

Sea Animals

Octopus

A sea animal with eight tentacles, two eyes. It is a mollusk and an invertebrate, which means it has no bones in the body. There are more than 150 types of octopus.

The Dolphin

Dolphins are small members of the whale order, Cetacea. Dolphins are mammals and are noted for their intelligence and learning abilities.

Starfish

Sea stars or commonly known as starfish are marine animals that have a central body with rays. Starfishes are not fishes since they do not have backbones and are called invertebrate.

Turtles

Sea turtles are the turtles that live in the world's oceans. There are seven species, and they are split into two families: the Dermochelyidae and the Cheloniidae.

Elephant Seals

Elephant seals are the largest members of the group of aquatic, fin-footed mammals called pinnipeds.

Fish

The word fish is often used to describe many animals that live in water. Worldwide nearly 1,200 species of fish have been identified as threatened with extinction.

Sea Horse

Nothing more unlike a fish could be imagined that the sea horse. In fact it looks much like the knight in a chess game. The sea horse has a head of and neck shaped like a horse, and it swims in an upright position.

Crabs

Crabs are short-tailed crustaceans that may live either on land or in the sea. Many species, including the blue (Callinectes sapidus), Dungeness (Cancer magister), and king (Paralithodes camtschatica) crabs, are eaten buy humans.

Write down and draw other Sea Animals you know.

Write down and draw other Sea Animals you know.

Desert Animals

Snakes

Of all the animals, snakes are among the best known but perhaps the most misunderstood. Snakes are characterized by their elongated limbless bodies.

Fennec

A small pale fox with large pointed ears, native to the deserts of North Africa and Arabia.

Camel

The two species of large hoofed animals known as camels were domesticated about 4,000 to 5,000 years ago. Ever since, they have provided meat, milk, wool, and hides to various desert- and mountain-dwelling peoples of the Eastern and Western Hemispheres.

Write down and draw other Desert Animals you know.

Write down and draw other Desert Animals you know.

Forest Animals

Bear

Bears are large, powerful mammals related to dogs and raccoons. The biggest bears are the world's largest animals that live on land and eat meat.

Fox

Foxes are mammals that look like small, bushy-tailed dogs. They live all over the world. Different kinds favor different habitats.

Wild Boar

Wild boar is a specie of wild pig, native to the forests of Europe, north-west of Africa and also found throughout Asia.

Hedgehog

When the spiny hedgehog is frightened or attacked, it rolls itself into a ball to protect its vulnerable face and underparts, exposing only its sharp prickly spines.

Squirrels

A small animal with a long tail and soft fur that lives in trees. They usually eat nuts.

Deer

Members of the deer family are found throughout the Western Hemisphere, Europe and Asia.

Wolf

Believed to be an ancestor of the domestic dog, the wolf is a highly intelligent and courageous hunter. Its remarkable powers of endurance are legendary.

Woodpecker

When a woodpecker drums a tree, it is usually looking for a food. Once it has detected the sounds of insects gnawing or moving withing the wood, it begins to hammer persistently in pursuit of its prey.

Write down and draw other Forest Animals you know.

Write down and draw other Forest Animals you know.

Made in the USA
Lexington, KY
26 September 2017